WEEKLY WR READER®
EARLY LEARNING LIBRARY

WHY ANIMALS LOOK DIFFERENT

Animal Tails

Jonatha A. Brown

Reading consultant: Susan Nations, M.Ed., author/literacy coach/
consultant in literacy development
Science and curriculum consultant: Debra Voege, M.A., science
and math curriculum resource teacher

Please visit our web site at: www.garethstevens.com
For a free color catalog describing Weekly Reader® Early Learning Library's list
of high-quality books, call 1-877-445-5824 (USA) or 1-800-387-3178 (Canada).
Weekly Reader® Early Learning Library's fax: (414) 336-0164.

Library of Congress Cataloging-in-Publication Data

Brown, Jonatha A.
  Animal tails / by Jonatha A. Brown.
    p. cm. — (Why animals look different)
  Includes bibliographical references and index.
  ISBN-10: 0-8368-6863-3 – ISBN-13: 978-0-8368-6863-0 (lib. bdg.)
  ISBN-10: 0-8368-6868-4 – ISBN-13: 978-0-8368-6868-5 (softcover)
  1. Tail—Juvenile literature. I. Title. II. Series: Brown, Jonatha A.
  Why animals look different.
  QL950.6.B76   2007
  573.9'9833—dc22   2006010979

This edition first published in 2007 by
Weekly Reader® Early Learning Library
A Member of the WRC Media Family of Companies
330 West Olive Street, Suite 100
Milwaukee, WI 53212 USA

Editor: Gini Holland
Art direction: Tammy West
Cover design and page layout: Charlie Dahl
Picture research: Diane Laska-Swanke

Picture credits: Cover, title, © Wendy Dennis/Visuals Unlimited; p. 4 © Steve Maslowski/Visuals Unlimited; p. 5 © Brandon Cole/Visuals Unlimited; p. 6 © Richard Du Toit/naturepl.com; pp. 7, 15 © Michael H. Francis; p. 8 © Mark Carwardine/naturepl.com; p. 9 © Colin Seddon/naturepl.com; p. 10 © Ken Lucas/Visuals Unlimited; p. 11 © Jeffrey L. Rotman/CORBIS; p. 12 © Stuart Westmorland/CORBIS; p. 13 © Peter Scoones/naturepl.com; p. 14 © Gerald & Buff Corsi/Visuals Unlimited; p. 16 © Jim Merli/Visuals Unlimited; p. 17 © Pete Oxford/naturepl.com; p. 18 © Mark Payne-Gill/naturepl.com; p. 19 © William Weber/Visuals Unlimited; p. 20 © Sharon Heald/naturepl.com; p. 21 © Tom and Pat Leeson

Printed in the United States of America

1 2 3 4 5 6 7 8 9 10 09 08 07 06

Table of Contents

Cover and title page: The ring-tailed lemur uses its tail like a flag. The lemur waves its tail to show other lemurs where it is.

Bottoms Up!

Different animals have different kinds of tails. Cheetahs have tails that work for steering. Dolphins have tails that work for swimming. Porcupines have tails that can be used as **weapons**. Opossums have tails that can hold on to tree branches.

The opossum can hang from its tail! Now the opossum can reach food or another branch with its front feet.

The way an animal's tail looks depends on what the tail is used for. The dolphin has a broad, flat tail for swimming. Opossums' thin tails help them hold on to things. Each animal has the kind of tail it needs.

Dolphins swim by moving their broad, flat tails up and down.

Cheetahs have long tails. They use their tails to steer when they run.

Steering and Balance

Cheetahs and mountain lions are fast runners. When a big cat's **prey** makes a sharp turn to try to escape, the cat needs to turn quickly, too. It swings its long tail to the side to steer its body through the turn.

Otters and beavers use their tails to steer when they swim. Both animals sweep their tails to the side to turn in the water. On land, beavers lean on their tails when they stand on their hind legs. This helps them **balance**.

Otters use their tails to swim. This swimming otter can swing its tail to the side to steer.

This standing penguin is using its tail for balance. A stiff tail helps keep the penguin from falling over backwards.

Other animals use their tails for balance, too. The kangaroo balances on its long, thick tail as it stands and hops. The penguin balances on its two short legs and its short, stiff tail feathers when it stands.

Even mice use their tails for balance. Most mice have long tails for their size. When they walk, run, and climb, they carry their tails out behind them for balance. They can also drape their tails around thin plant stems so they do not fall over.

This mouse has wrapped its tail around some twigs. This keeps the mouse from falling off a thin stem.

A catfish looks for bits of food in a river. A rounded tail lets the catfish swim slowly as it is looking for food.

Swimming with Tails

Fish use their tails to swim. Catfish swim slowly along the bottoms of rivers and lakes as they gather food. The catfish has a rounded tail. This tail shape is good for slow swimming and for short bursts of speed.

The swordfish feeds on tuna and other fish in the ocean. It needs to swim fast to catch its prey. The tail of the swordfish has a curved part on the end, shaped like a **crescent** moon. This tail shape works well for swimming straight and fast.

The end of a swordfish's tail is curved. This tail shape helps the swordfish swim fast.

A whale moves its broad, flat tail up and down to swim.

Some whales swim far north and south as the seasons change. Their broad, flat tails are made for swimming long distances. Whales and dolphins do not move their tails back and forth as fish do. They move them up and down in big, powerful **strokes**.

Alligators also use their tails to swim. Their tails are thick, flat, and very long. They swim by moving their tails back and forth. Alligators can move their tails the same way when they crawl. Their tails push them forward in water.

This alligator swings its tail back and forth to swim. Alligators are strong swimmers.

Tail Defense

Some animals use their tails as weapons. The tail of a porcupine is covered with sharp quills. When an animal attacks it, the porcupine swings its tail back and forth. The porcupine's enemy usually leaves the fight with quills stuck deep in its skin.

The porcupine has many sharp quills in its tail. These quills can hurt another animal very badly.

14

Biting flies sometimes attack horses. When flies bite, horses swish their tails back and forth to swat them off. Horses can reach the whole back half of their bodies with their tails. Giraffes and zebras use their tails as flyswatters, too.

This horse is using its tail as a flyswatter. The horse is trying to brush flies off its skin.

Some lizards can drop their tails. When an enemy attacks it, the lizard's tail breaks off. The tail lies twitching on the ground as the lizard tries to run away! If the lizard escapes, its tail can grow back.

This lizard's tail may have broken off in a fight with another animal.

Terrific Tails!

Spider monkeys and opossums live in trees. Their tails can wrap around branches and hold on tightly. A spider monkey can hang from a tree branch by its tail while it reaches for fruit to eat.

A spider monkey's tail works almost like a hand for holding things tightly.

This fox is trying to stay warm on a cold day. The fox uses its long, fluffy tail to cover its nose.

Furry tails can help animals stay warm. Squirrels use their tails to **protect** their backs and heads from cold winds. Foxes sleep with their fluffy tails over their faces. Snow leopards wrap their tails around their bodies and necks for warmth.

Some male birds use their tails to **attract** mates. Male peacocks spread their colorful tails to show females that they are big and healthy. Male turkeys spread their tails in the same way. Both kinds of birds use their tails to show off.

A male peacock spreads its big, beautiful tail to show off to a female.

This lizard has stored fat and water in its tail. This allows the lizard to live for many days without food and water.

Many lizards live in hot, dry places. These animals store water and fat in their tails. If they drop their tails in a fight, they lose this stored fat and water. They may die from lack of food or water before a new tail grows.

Some birds use their tails as **brakes**. When an eagle lands, it drops and spreads its wide tail to slow its flight.

Animals have many different kinds of tails. Each one has the tail it needs for the way it lives.

This eagle has spread its tail to land on a branch. The eagle's wide tail helps slow the bird down when it lands.

Glossary

attract – get the attention or interest of

balance – keeping steady so as not to fall over

brakes – parts used to slow or stop a moving thing

crescent – curved like the outline of a new moon

prey – an animal that is hunted for food

protect – keep safe

strokes – sweeping motions that move an animal through water or across snow or ice

weapons – tools used for fighting

For More Information

Books

Salamanders And Other Animals With Amazing Tails. Scholastic News Nonfiction Readers (series). Susan Labella. (Children's Press)

Tails That Talk And Fly. Up Close (series). Diane Swanson. (Sterling)

Terrific Tails. Hana Machotka. (William Morrow)

Web Sites

Fun Facts About Bottlenose Dolphins

www.dolphin-institute.org/resource_guide/kids/tdidream/objectives.htm
Click on different parts of the dolphin's body to learn how it helps the dolphin survive.

Penguin Activities

www.kidzone.ws/animals/penguins/activities.htm
Learn cool facts, and enjoy penguin riddles and puzzles.

Index

About the Author

Jonatha A. Brown has written many nonfiction books for children. She lives in Phoenix, Arizona, with her husband, Warren, and their two dogs, Sasha and Ava. Jonatha also has two horses, Fleetwood and Freedom. She would have more animals if Warren would only let her! They both enjoy watching coyotes, rabbits, ground squirrels, lizards, and birds in their backyard.